THE EVOLUTION OF AN EMPIRE

A Brief Historical Sketch Of France

By

MARY PLATT PARMELE

The Evolution of An Empire
A Brief Historical Sketch Of France

by **Mary Platt Parmele**

ISBN: 978-93-57487-94-8

Published by

DOUBLE 9 BOOKS
2/13-B, Ansari Road, Daryaganj
New Delhi – 110002
info@double9books.com
www.double9books.com
Tel. 011-40042856

ABOUT THE AUTHOR

Author and historian Mary Platt Parmele lived in America from 1843 until 1911. She was an American scholar and historian who was born in Mary Platt Parmele (1843-1911). She was raised in New Haven, where her father was a professor at Yale University, after being born in Stratford, Connecticut. In New York City, Parmele started her writing career as an editor and writer for newspapers and magazines. Afterwards, she began producing historical works, among them A Short History of England, The Development of an Empire: A Historical Outline of Rome, and The Evolution of an Empire: A Quick Historical Sketch of France. Parmele's work was distinguished by its lucidity and accessibility to a broad readership. She tried to pique readers' interest in history who may not have been otherwise interested. Parmele supported women's rights to an education and the vote. She was active in several women's rights groups and served as president of the New York State Woman Suffrage Association. At the age of 67, Parmele passed away in 1911. Her contributions to historical writing contributed to the study of history's increased accessibility and popularity.

CONTENTS

CHAPTER I. 7

CHAPTER II. 11

CHAPTER III. 13

CHAPTER IV. 16

CHAPTER V. 20

CHAPTER VI. 23

CHAPTER VII. 26

CHAPTER VIII. 29

CHAPTER IX. 33

CHAPTER X. 36

CHAPTER XI. 40

CHAPTER XII. 44

CHAPTER I.

One of the greatest achievements of modern research is the discovery of a key by which we may determine the kinship of nations. What we used to conjecture, we now know. An identity in the structural form of language establishes with scientific certitude that however diverse their character and civilizations, Russian, German, English, French, Spaniard, are all but branches from the same parent stem, are all alike children of the Asiatic Aryan.

So skilful are modern methods of questioning the past, and so determined the effort to find out its secrets, we may yet know the origin and history of this wonderful Asiatic people, and when and why they left their native continent and colonized upon the northern shores of the Mediterranean. Certain it is, however, that, more centuries before the Christian era than there have been since, they had peopled Western Europe.

This branch of the Aryan family is known as the Keltic, and was older brother to the Teuton and Slav, which at a much later period followed them from the ancestral home, and appropriated the middle and eastern portions of the European Continent.

The name of Gaul was given to the territory lying between the Ocean and the Mediterranean, and the Pyrenees and the Alps. And at a later period a portion of Northern Gaul, and the islands lying north of it, received from an invading chieftain and his tribe the name *Brit* or *Britain* (or Pryd or Prydain).

If the mind could be carried back on the track of time, and we could see what we now call France as it existed twenty centuries before the Christian era, we should behold the same natural features: the same mountains rearing their heads; the same rivers flowing to the sea; the same plains stretching out in the sunlight. But instead of vines and flowers and cultivated fields we should behold great herds of wild ox and elk, and of swine as fierce as wolves, ranging in a climate as cold as Norway; and vast inaccessible forests, the home of beasts of prey, which contended with man for food and shelter.

Let us read Guizot's description of life in Gaul five centuries before Christ:

"Here lived six or seven millions of men a bestial life, in dwellings dark and low, built of wood and clay and covered with branches or straw, open to daylight by the door alone and confusedly heaped together behind a rampart of timber, earth, and stone, which enclosed and protected what they were pleased to call—a *town*."

Such was the Paris, and such the Frenchmen of the age of Pericles! And the same tides that washed the sands of Southern Gaul, a few hours later ebbed and flowed upon the shores of Greece—rich in culture, with refinements and subtleties in art which are the despair of the world to-day— with an intellectual endowment never since attained by any people.

The same sun which rose upon temples and palaces and life serene and beautiful in Greece, an hour later lighted sacrificial altars and hideous orgies in the forests of Gaul. While the Gaul was nailing the heads of human victims to his door, or hanging them from the bridle of his horse, or burning or flogging his prisoners to death, the Greek, with a literature, an art, and a civilization in ripest perfection, discussed with his friends the deepest problems of life and destiny, which were then baffling human intelligence, even as they are with us to-day. Truly we of Keltic and Teuton descent are late-comers upon the stage of national life.

There was no promise of greatness in ancient Gaul. It was a great unregulated force, rushing hither and thither. Impelled by insatiate greed for the possessions of their neighbors, there was no permanence in their loves or their hatreds. The enemies of to-day were the allies of to-morrow. Guided entirely by the fleeting desires and passions of the moment, with no far-reaching plans to restrain, the sixty or more tribes composing the Gallic people were in perpetual state of feud and anarchy, apparently insensible to the ties of brotherhood, which give concert of action, and stability in form of national life. If they overran a neighboring country, it seemed not so much for permanent acquisition, as to make it a camping-ground until its resources were exhausted.

We read of one Massillia who came with a colony of Greeks long ages ago, and after founding the city of Marseilles, created a narrow bright border of Greek civilization along the Southern edge of the benighted land. It was a brief illumination, lasting only a century or more, and leaving few traces; but it may account for the superior intellectual quality of the southern provinces in future France.

It requires a vast extent of territory to sustain a people living by the chase, and upon herds and flocks; hence the area which now amply maintains thirty-five millions of Frenchmen was all too small for six or seven million Gauls; and they were in perpetual struggle with their neighbors for land— more land.

"Give us land," they said to the Romans, and when land was denied them and the gates of cities disdainfully closed upon their messengers, not land, but vengeance, was their cry; and hordes of half-naked barbarians trampled down the vineyards, and rushed, a tumultuous torrent, upon Rome.

The Romans could not stand before this new and strange kind of warfare. The Gauls streamed over the vanquished legions into the Eternal City, silent and deserted save only by the Senate and a few who remained intrenched in the Citadel; and there the barbarians kept them besieged for seven months, while they made themselves at home amid uncomprehended luxuries.

Of course Roman skill and courage at last dislodged and drove them back. But the fact remained that the Gaul had been there, — master of Rome; that the ironclad legions had been no match for his naked force, and a new sensation thrilled through the length and breadth of Gaul. It was the first throb of national life. The sixty or more fragments drew closer together into something like Gallic unity — with a common danger to meet, a common foe to drive back.

Hereafter there was another hunger to be appeased besides that for food and land; a hunger for conquest, for vengeance, and for glory for the Gallic name. National pride was born.

For years they hovered like wolves about Rome. But skill and superior intelligence tell in the centuries. It took long — and cost no end of blood and treasure; but two hundred years from the capture of Rome, the Gauls were driven out of Italy, and the Alps pronounced a barrier set by Nature herself against barbarian encroachments.

Italy was not the only country suffering from the destroying footsteps of the Western Kelts. There had been long ago an overflow of a tribe in Northern Gaul (the Kymrians), which had hewed and plundered its way south and eastward; until at the time of Alexander (340 B.C.) it was knocking at the gates of Macedonia.

Stimulated by the success at Rome fifty years earlier, they were, with fresh insolence, demanding "land," and during the centuries which followed, the Gallic name acquired no fresh lustre in Greece. Half-naked, gross, ferocious and ignorant, sometimes allies, but always a scourge, they finally crossed the Hellespont (278 B.C.), and turned their attention to Asia Minor. And there, at last, we find them settled in a province called Gallicia, where they lived without amalgamating with the people about them; it is said, even as late as 400 years after Christ, speaking the language of their tribal home (what is now Belgium). And these were the Galatians — the "foolish Galatians," to whom Paul addressed his epistle; and we have followed up this Gallic thread simply because it mingles with the larger strand of ancient and sacred history with which we are all so familiar.

It is not strange that Roman courage and endurance became a by-word. Her fibre was toughened by perpetual strain of conflict. Even while she was struggling with Gaul and while the echoes of the Hunnish invasion were still resounding through the Continent, Hannibal, with his hosts, was pouring through Gaul and gathering accessions from that people as he swept down into Italy. Then, with the memories of the Carthagenian wars still fresh at Rome, the Goths were at her gates,—their blows directed with a solidity superior to that of the barbarians who had preceded them. Where the Gauls had knocked, the Goths thundered.

Again the city was invaded by barbarian feet, and again did superior training and intelligence drive back the invading torrent and triumph over native brute force.

Such, in brief outline, was the condition of the centuries just before the Christian era.

CHAPTER II.

The making of a nation is not unlike bread or cake making. One element is used as the basis, to which are added other component parts, of varying qualities, and the result we call England, or Germany, or France. The steps by which it is accomplished, the blending and fusing of the elements, require centuries, and the process makes what we call — history.

It was written in the book of fate that Gaul should become a great nation; but not until fused and interpenetrated with two other nationalities. She must first be humanized and civilized by the Roman, and then energized and made free from the Roman by the Teuton.

The instrument chosen for the former was Julius Cæsar, and for the latter — five centuries later — Clovis, the Frankish leader. It is safe to affirm that no man has ever so changed the course of human events as did Julius Cæsar. Napoleon, who strove to imitate him 1800 years later, was a charlatan in comparison; a mere scene-shifter on a great theatrical stage. Not a trace of his work remains upon humanity to-day.

Cæsar opened up a pathway for the old civilizations of the world to flow into Western Europe, and the sodden mass of barbarism was infused with a life-compelling current. This was not accomplished by placing before the inferior race a higher ideal of life for imitation, but by a mingling of the blood of the nations — a transfusion into Gallic veins of the germs of a higher living and thinking — thus making them heirs to the great civilizations of antiquity.

No human event was ever fraught with such consequences to the human race as the conquest of Gaul by Julius Cæsar.

The Gallic wars had for centuries drained the treasure and taxed the resources of Rome. Cæsar conceived the audacious idea of stopping them at their source — in fact, of making Gaul a Roman province.

It was a marvellous exhibition, not simply of force, but of force wielded by supreme intelligence and craft. He had lived four years among this people and knew their sources of weakness, their internal jealousies and rivalries, their incohesiveness. When they hurled themselves against Rome, it was as a mass of sharp fragments. When the Goths did the same, it was as one solid, indivisible body. Cæsar saw that by adroit management he could disintegrate this people, even while conquering them.

By forcibly maintaining in power those who submitted to him, being by turns gentle and severe, ingratiating here, terrifying there, he established a tremendous personal force; and during nine years carried on eight campaigns, marvels in the art of war, as well as in the subtler methods of negotiation and intrigue. He had successively dealt with all the Gallic tribes, even including Great Britain, subjugating either through their own rivalries, or by his invincible arm.

Equally able to charm and to terrify, he had all the gifts, all the means to success and empire, that can be possessed by man. Great in politics as in war, as full of resource in the forum as on the battle-field, he was by nature called to dominion.

It was not as a patriot, simply intent upon freeing Rome of an harassing enemy, that he endured those nine years in Gaul—not as a great leader burning with military ardor that he conducted those eight campaigns. The conquest of Gaul meant the greater conquest of Rome. The one was accomplished; he now turned his back upon the devastated country, and prepared to complete his great project of human ascendency.

Rome was mistress of the world; he—would be master of Rome.

CHAPTER III.

While the Star of Empire was thus moving toward the West, another and brighter star was about to arise in the East. So accustomed are we to the story, that we lose all sense of wonder at its recital.

Julius Cæsar's brief triumph was over. Marc Antony had recited his virtues over his bier, Rome had wept, and then forgotten him in the absorbing splendors of his nephew Augustus. In an obscure village of an obscure country in Asia Minor, the young wife of a peasant finds shelter in a stable, and gives birth to a son, who is cradled in the straw of a manger, from which the cattle are feeding.

Can the mind conceive of human circumstances more lowly? The child grew to manhood, and in his thirty-three years of life was never lifted above the obscure sphere into which he was born; never spoke from the vantage-ground of worldly elevation,—simply moving among people of his own station in life, mechanics, fishermen, and peasants, he told of a religion of love, a gospel of peace, for which he was willing to die.

Who would have dreamed that this was the germ of the most potent, the most regenerative force the world had ever known? That thrones, empires, principalities, and powers would melt and crumble before his name? Of all miracles, is not this the greatest?

The passionate ardor with which this religion was propagated in the first two centuries had no motive but the yearning to make others share in its benefits and hopes; and to this end to accept the belief that Jesus Christ had come in fulfilment of a long-promised Saviour,—who should be sent to this world clothed with divine authority to establish a spiritual kingdom, in which he was King of Kings, Lord of Lords, Mediator between us and the Father, of whom he was the "only begotten Son."

The religion in its essence was absolutely simple. Its founder summed it up in two sentences,—expressing the duty of man to man, and of man to God. That was all the Theology he formulated.

For two centuries the religion of Christ was an elementary spiritual force. It appealed only to the highest attributes and longings of the human soul, and under its sustaining influence frail women, men, and even children were able to endure tortures, of which we cannot read even now without shuddering horror.

Nature's method of gardening is very beautiful. She carefully guards the seed until it is ripe, then she bursts the imprisoning walls and gives it to the winds to distribute. Precisely such method was used in disseminating Christianity. It was not for one people — it was for the healing of the nations, and its home was wherever man abides.

Nearly five decades after Christ's death upon the cross, Jerusalem was destroyed by Titus. The home of Christianity was effaced. At just the right moment the enclosing walls had broken, and freed to the winds the germs in all their primitive purity.

Imperial favor had not tarnished it, human ambitions had not employed and degraded it, nor had it been made into complex system by ingenious casuists. The pure spiritual truth, unsullied as it came from the hand of its founder, was scattered broadcast, as the band of Christians dispersed throughout the Roman Empire, naturally forming into communities here and there, which became the centres of Christian propagandism. Lyons in Gaul was such a centre.

The fires of persecution had been lighted here and there throughout the Empire, and the Emperor Nero, under whom the Apostles Peter and Paul are said to have suffered martyrdom, had amused himself by making torches of the Christians at Rome. But until 177 A.D. Gaul was exempt from such horrors.

Marcus Aurelius — that peerless pagan, — large in intelligence, exalted in character, and guided by a conscientious rectitude which has made his name shine like a star in the lurid light of Roman history, still failed utterly to comprehend the significance of this spiritual kingdom established by Christ on earth. He it was who ordered the first persecution in Gaul. In pursuance of his command, horrible tortures were inflicted at Lyons upon those who would not abjure the new faith.

A letter, written by an eye-witness, pictures with terrible vividness the scenes which followed. Many cases are described with harrowing detail, and of one Blandina it is said: "From morn till eve they put her to all manner of torture, marvelling that she still lived with her body pierced through and through and torn piecemeal by so many tortures of which a single one should have sufficed to kill her, to which she only replied, 'I am a Christian.'"

The recital goes on to tell how she was then cast into a dungeon, — her feet compressed and dragged out to the utmost tension of the muscles, — then left alone in darkness, until new methods of torture could be devised.

Finally she was brought, with other Christians, into the amphitheatre, hanging from a cross to which she was tied, and there thrown to the beasts. As the beasts refused to touch her she was taken back to the dungeon to be reserved for another occasion, being brought out daily to witness the fate and suffering of her friends and fellow-martyrs; still answering the oft-repeated question—"I am a Christian."

The writer goes on to say, "After she had undergone fire, the talons of beasts, and every agony which could be thought of, she was wrapped in a network and thrown to a bull, who tossed her in the air"—and her sufferings were ended.

Truly it cost something to say "I am a Christian" in those days.

Marcus Aurelius probably gave orders for the persecution at Lyons, with little knowledge of what would be the nature of those persecutions, or of the religion he was trying to exterminate. Some of the hours spent in writing introspective essays would have been well employed in studying the period in which he lived, and the Empire he ruled.

Paganism and Druidism, those twin monsters, receded before the advancing light of Christianity. Neither contained anything which could nourish the soul of man, and both had become simply badges of nationality.

Druidism was the last stronghold of independent Gallic life. It was a mixture of northern myth and oriental dreams of metempsychosis, coarse, mystical, and cruel. The Roman paganism which was superimposed by the conquering race was the mere shell of a once vital religion. Educated men had long ceased to believe in the gods and divinities of Greece,

In the year 312, alas for Christianity, it was espoused by imperial power. When the Emperor Constantine declared himself a Christian, there was no doubt rejoicing among the saints; but it was the beginning of the degeneracy of the religion of Christ. The faith of the humble was to be raised to a throne; its lowly garb to be exchanged for purple and scarlet, the gospel of peace to be enforced by the sword.

The Empire was crumbling, and upon its ruins the race of the future and social conditions of modern times were forming. Paganism and Druidism would have been an impossibility. Christianity even with its lustre dimmed, its purity tarnished, its simplicity overlaid with scholasticism, was better than these. The miracle had been accomplished. The great Roman Empire had said: "I am Christian."

CHAPTER IV.

Gaul had been Latinized and Christianized. Now one more thing was needed to prepare her for a great future. Her fibre was to be toughened by the infusion of a stronger race. Julius Cæsar had shaken her into submission, and Rome had chastised her into decency of behavior and speech, but as her manners improved her native vigor declined. She took kindly to Roman luxury and effeminacy, and could no longer have thundered at the gates of her neighbors demanding "land."

But at last the great Roman Empire was dying, and even degenerate Gaul was struggling out of her relaxing grasp. In her extremity she called upon the Franks, a powerful Germanic race, to aid her. This people had long looked with covetous eyes at the fair fields stretching beyond the Rhine, and lost no time in accepting the invitation. They overspread the land, and Gaul and Roman alike were submerged beneath the Teuton flood, while the Frankish Conqueror, Clovis (son of the great Merovaæus), was at Paris (or "Lutetia") wearing the kingly crown.

Such was the beginning of independent and of dynastic life in France.

Rome had found a more powerful ally than she hoped; and the desire of Gaul was accomplished in that she was free from Rome. But the king of whom she had dreamed was of her own race; not this terrible Frank. Had she exchanged one servitude for another? Had she been, not set free, but simply annexed to the realm of the Barbarian across the Rhine? Let us say rather that it was an espousal. She had brought her dowry of beauty and "land," that most coveted of possessions, and had pledged obedience, for which she was to be cherished, honored, and protected, and to bear the name of her lord.

*****

Ancient heroes are said to be seen through a shadowy lens, which magnifies their stature. Let us hope that the crimes of the three or four generations immediately succeeding Clovis have been in like manner expanded; for it is sickening to read of such monstrous prodigality of wickedness. Whole families butchered, husbands, wives, children — anything obstructing the path to the throne — with an atrocity which makes Richard III.

seem a mere pigmy in the art of intrigue and killing. The chapter closes with the daughter and mother of kings (Brunehilde or Brunhaut) naked and tied by one arm, one leg and her hair to the tail of an unbroken horse, and amid jeers and shouts dashed over the stones of Paris (600 A.D.).

But even the Frank succumbed to the enervating Gallic influence. The Merovingian line commenced by Clovis faded from ferocity into imbecility. Its Kings in less than two centuries had become mere lay-figures, wearing the symbols of an authority which existed nowhere, unless in the *Maire du Palais*.

This office from being a sort of royal stewardship had grown to be the governing power *de facto*. While Theodoric, the Phantom King, was having his long locks dressed and perfumed, his *Maire du Palais*, Charles, was moulding and welding his kingdom, and at the same time staying the Mohammedan flood which was pouring over the Pyrenees; and, by his final and decisive blow in defence of the Christianity espoused by Clovis, earning the name *Charles Martel* (the hammer).

*****

Less than one hundred years after the death of Clovis, there had come out of Asia, that birthplace of religions, a new faith, which was destined to be for centuries the scourge of Christendom, and which to-day rules one-third of the human family. Zoroaster, Buddha, Christ, had successively come with saving message to humanity, and now (600 A.D.) Mohammed believed himself divinely appointed to drive out of Arabia the idolatry of ancient Magianism (the religion of Zoroaster).

Christianity had passed through strange vicissitudes. Kings, Emperors, Popes, and Bishops had been terrible custodians of its truths, and while many still held it in its primitive purity, ecclesiastics were fiercely fighting over the nature of the Trinity, the divinity of the Virgin Mother, and the Church was shaken to its foundation by furious factions.

In this hour of weakness, the Persians (590 A.D.) had conquered Asia Minor. Bethlehem, Gethsemane, and Calvary were profaned; the Holy Sepulchre had been burned, and the cross carried off amid shouts of laughter. Magianism had insulted Christianity, and no miracle had interposed! The heavens did not roll asunder, nor did the earth open her abysses to swallow them up. There was consternation and doubt in Christendom.

Such was the state of the Church when Mohammedanism came into existence. "There is but one God, and Mohammed is his Prophet." Such was its battle-cry and its creed, and the moral precepts of the Koran its gospel. There seems nothing in this to account for the mad enthusiasm and the passion for worship in its followers. But in less than a hundred years this lion out of Arabia had subjected Syria, Mesopotamia, Egypt, Northern Africa, and the Spanish Peninsula. Now, sword in one hand, and the Koran in the other, the Mohammedan had crossed the Pyrenees and was in Southern Gaul.

Under the strange magic of this faith, the largest religious empire the world had known had sprung into existence, stretching from the Chinese Wall to the Atlantic; from the Caspian to the Indian Ocean; and Jerusalem, the metropolis of Christianity-Jerusalem, the Mecca of the Christian, was lost! The crescent floated over the birthplace of our Lord, and notwithstanding the temporary successes of the Crusades, it does to this day.

If the Pyrenees were passed, the very existence of Christendom was threatened. Charles Martel, the grandfather of Charlemagne, averted this danger when he stayed the infidel flood at the battle of Tours, 732 A.D.

Pepin, the son of Charles Martel, who succeeded him as *Maire du Palais*, does not seem to have had the temper or spirit of an usurper, but simply to have been an energetic, resolute man who was bored by the circumlocution of governing through a King who did not exist. He determined to put an end to the fiction, and to cut the Gordian knot by first cutting the long curls of the last Merovingian, Childeric; and then putting the crown upon his own head, he sent the unfortunate phantom of royalty to a monastery, to reflect upon the uncertainty of human pleasures and events. By right of manhood and superiority, the Carlovingian line had succeeded to the Merovingian.

*****

Against the dark background of European history, and with the broad level of obscurity stretching over the ages at its feet, there rises one shining pinnacle. Considered as man or sovereign, Charlemagne is one of the most impressive figures in history. His seven feet of stature clad in shining steel, his masterful grasp of the forces of his time, his splendid intelligence, instinct even then with the modern spirit, all combine to elevate him in solitary grandeur.

Charlemagne found France in disorder measureless, and apparently insurmountable. Barbarian invasion without, and anarchy within; Saxon paganism pressing in upon the North, and Asiatic Islamism upon the South and West; a host of forces struggling for dominion in a nation brutish, ignorant, and without cohesion.

It is the attribute of genius to discern opportunity where others see nothing. Charlemagne saw rising out of this chaos a great resuscitated Roman empire, which should be at the same time a spiritual and Christian empire as well. Saxons, Slavs, Huns, Lombards, Arabs, came under his compelling grasp; these antagonistic races all held together by the force of one terrible will, in unnatural combination with France. No political liberties, no popular assemblies discussing public measures; it is Charlemagne alone who fills the picture; it is absolutism,—marked by prudence, ability, and grandeur, but still, absolutism.

The Pope looked approvingly upon this son of the Church by whose order 4,500 pagan heads could be cut off in one day, and a whole army compelled to baptism in an afternoon. Here was a champion to be propitiated! Charlemagne, on the other hand, saw in the Church the most compliant and effective means to empire. In the loving alliance formed, he was to be the protector, the Pope the protected. He wore the Church as a precious jewel in his crown.

It was a splendid dream, splendidly realized; the most imposing of human successes, and the most impressive of human failures. It seems designed as a lesson for the human race in the transitory nature of power applied from without.

The vast fabric passed with himself; was gone like a shadow when he was gone. The unity of the Empire was buried in the grave of its founder. In twenty-nine years (by the treaty of Verdun) three kingdoms emerged from the crumbling mass. France, Italy, Germany, already separated by race repulsions, had taken up each a distinct national existence, the Imperial crown remaining with Germany.

And France—France, the centre of this dream of unity, with her native incohesiveness, and in the irony of fate, had broken into no less than 59 fragments, loosely held together by one Carlovingian King.

CHAPTER V.

I think that it was Lincoln who said that "the Lord must like common people, because he had made so many of them." The path for the common people in France at this time led through heavy shadows. But a darker time was approaching. A system of oppression was maturing, which was soon to envelop them in the obscurity of darkest night.

Those Scandinavian freebooters called Northmen, and later Normans, were the scourge of the kingdom. Nothing was safe from their insolent courage and rapacity.

The rich could intrench themselves in stone fortresses, with moats and drawbridges, and be in comparative security, but the poor were utterly defenceless against this perennial destroyer. The result was a compact between the powerful and the weak, which was the beginning of the Feudal System. It was in effect an exchange of protection for service and fealty. You give us absolute control of your persons — your military service when required, and a portion of your substance and the fruit of your toil — and we will in exchange give you our fortified castles as a refuge from the Northmen. Such was the offer. It was a choice between vassalage, serfdom, or destruction outright.

Simple enough in its beginnings, this became a ramified system of oppression, a curious network of authority, ingeniously controlling an entire people. The conditions upon which was engrafted this compact were of great antiquity, had indeed been brought across the Rhine by their German conquerors; but the Northmen were the impelling cause of the swift development of feudalism in France.

Charlemagne had felt grave apprehensions of evil from these robber incursions, but could not have conceived of a result such as this, the most oppressive system ever fastened upon a nation, and one which would at the same time sap the foundations of royalty itself.

The theory was that the King was absolute owner of all the territory; the great lords holding their titles from him on condition of military service, their vassals pledging military service and obedience to them again on similar terms, and sub-vassals again to them repeating the pledge; and so on in descending chain, until at last the serf, that wretched being whom none looks up to nor fears, is ground to powder beneath the superimposed mass. No appeal from the authority, no escape from the caprice or cruelty of his feudal lord. Could any scales weigh, could any words measure the suffering which must have been endured? Is it strange, with every aspiration thwarted, hope stifled, that Europe sank into the long sleep of the Middle Ages?

It is easy to conceive that under such a system, where all the affairs of the realm were adjusted by individual rulers with unlimited power, and where the great barons could make war upon each other without authorization from the King, that by the time this nominal head of the entire system was reached, there was nothing for him to do. In fact, there was not left one vestige of kingly authority, and Carlovingian rulers were almost as insignificant as their Merovingian predecessors. France had, instead of one great sovereign, 150 petty ones!

*****

In 911 A.D. the Northmen were offered the province henceforth known as Normandy, upon condition of their acceptance of the religion and submission to the laws of the realm. Rollo, the disreputable robber-chief, took the oath of fealty to the King of France his Suzerain, and Christian baptism transformed him into respectable, law-abiding Robert, Duke of Normandy.

With marvellous facility this people took on the language and manners of their neighbors, and in a century and a half were prepared to instruct the Britons in a higher civilization.

I think it is one hundred years of respectability that is required by a certain aristocratic club for admission to its membership. The blood does not acquire the proper shade of azure until it has flowed in the full light of day for at least three generations. Decidedly, William the Conqueror, first Norman King of England, could not have been admitted to this club.

A century before his birth, his ancestors had lived by looting their neighbors. They were highwaymen, robbers, by profession. And, to increase his ineligibility, his mother, a pretty Norman peasant girl, daughter of a tanner, had ensnared the affections of that pleasant Duke of Normandy, known as "Robert the Devil."

William, the fruit of this unconsecrated union, became in time Duke of Normandy. With that reversion to ancestral types to which scientists tell us we are all liable, he seems to have looked across the Channel toward England, with an awakening of his robber-instincts. In a few weeks, Harold, the last King of the Saxons, lay dead at his feet, and William, Duke of Normandy, was William I., King of England.

Then was presented the curious anomaly of an English sovereign who was also ruler of a French province; an English king who was vassal to the

King of France. A door was thus opened (1066 A.D.) through which entered entangling complications and countless woes in the future.

*****

If Charlemagne had worn the Church as a precious jewel in his crown in the ninth century, the Church now in the eleventh century wore all the European states, a tiara of jewels in her mitre. The centre of dominion had passed from the Empire of Germany to Rome, when Henry IV. prostrated himself barefooted before Gregory VII. at Canossa in 1072.

The Church was at its zenith. As a political system it was unrivalled; but its triumphs brought little joy to the earnest souls still clinging to the ideals of primitive Christianity. But what availed it for Abelard to lead an intellectual revolt against corrupted beliefs in the North, or the Albigenses a spiritual one in the South? He was silenced and immured for life, while the unhappy inhabitants of Languedoc were massacred and almost exterminated, and an inquisition, established at Toulouse, made sure that heretical germs should not again spread from that infected centre.

But however imperfect the religious sentiment of the time, however it may have departed from the simple precepts of its founder, its power to sway the hearts and lives of the people may be judged from the extraordinary movement started in France in the twelfth century.

How inconceivable, in this practical age, that Europe should three times have emptied her choicest and best into Asia for a sentiment! Business suspended, private interests sacrificed or forgotten, life, treasure, all eagerly given—for what? That a small bit of territory, a thousand miles away, be torn from profaning infidels, because of its sacred associations, because it was the birthplace of a religion whose meaning seems to have escaped them—a religion which they wore on their battle-flags, but not in their hearts. How would a barefooted, rope-girdled monk, however inspired and eloquent, fare to-day in New York, or London, or Paris?

History has no stranger chapter than that of the Crusades. When Peter the Hermit pictured the desecration of the Holy Land by Mohammedans, all classes in France, from King to serf, were for the first time moved by a common sentiment, and poured life and treasure with passionate zeal into those streams which three times inundated Palestine.

The order of Knights Templar had been created, and a splendid ideal of manhood held up before the French nation, and now the knightly ideal, side by side with the Christian and the romantic ideal, entered into the life of the people. Romance, song, poetry, eloquence came into being from a sort of spiritual baptism, and France began to wear the mantle of beauty which was to be her chief glory in the future.

But future France was not clad in coat of mail in the twelfth century. She was lying helpless, beneath the mass of feudal trappings. Her time was not yet.

CHAPTER VI.

Like all oppressive systems, feudalism bore within itself the seeds of its own destruction. When the King, shorn of prerogative and of dignity, made alliance with the people lying in helpless misery beneath the mailed surface, the system was rudely shaken. When artisans flocked to the free cities enjoying especial immunities and privileges from the King, and by skill and industry amassed fortunes, the *commune* and the *bourgeoisie* were created, and feudalism was stricken to its centre. When spendthrift nobles and needy barons mortgaged their estates, the end was not far off. And when in 1302 the *"tiers état"* entered the States-General as a legitimate order of the Government, the very foundations were crumbling, and it needed but the final *coup de grâce* given by Charles VII. in the fifteenth century, when he established a standing army under the control of the King. When this was done, the feudal system was relegated to the region of the obsolete.

It was well for that sovereign that he could do something to save his name from the obloquy attached to it on account of his base desertion of Joan of Arc, to whom he owed his throne and his kingdom.

From the moment when a French province was attached to the crown of England, the dream of that nation was the conquest of France. Generations came and went, one dynasty replaced another, and still the struggle continued; France sometimes seeming near to dominion over England, and England always believing it was her destiny to bring France under the rule of an English sovereign.

A glamour of romance is thrown over history by the royal marriages which occur in dazzling profusion. It seems to have been the custom, whenever a peace was concluded in Europe, to cement it with a royal marriage, and to throw in a princess as a sacrifice, — one of the conditions of almost every treaty being that a royal daughter, or sister, or niece, should be tossed across the Channel, or into Germany, or Italy, or Spain, an unwilling bride thrown into the arms of a reluctant bridegroom; with the result that in the succeeding generation there was a plentiful sprinkling of heirs with claims, more or less shadowy, to the neighboring thrones. This was the source, or rather pretext, for most of the wars between France and England for four hundred years.

In the early part of the fifteenth century the great crisis arrived. With that lack of unity which seemed a fatal Gallic inheritance, France broke into civil war, while an invading English army was in the heart of her kingdom. England's dream was near realization.

An insane King, a vicious intriguing Queen-Regent, the Duke of Burgundy madly jealous of the Duke of Orleans, and both ready to sacrifice France in the rage of disappointed ambition,—such were the elements. England's opportunity had come.

The depraved Queen Isabella, acting for her insane husband, held conference with Henry V., and actually concluded a treaty bestowing the regency upon the English King. There was the usual douceur of a princess thrown in, and Katharine, the daughter of Isabella, and sister to the Dauphin (the future King Charles VII.), was espoused by King Henry V. of England, who set up a royal court at Vincennes.

The fortunes of the kingdom had never been so desperate. The people saw in these insolent traitorous dukes their natural enemy; in the King, their friend and protector. Had not monarchy given them life and hope? It was to them sacred next to Heaven. They rose in an outburst of patriotism. The young Dauphin was hastily and informally crowned, and thousands flocked to his standard. It was the King and the people against the great vassals, the last struggle of an expiring feudalism. Desperation lent fury to the conflict which was, upon both sides, a fight for existence; the Queen-mother in unnatural alliance with the Duke of Burgundy, who was resolved to rule or ruin.

He soon saw that defeat was inevitable, and, preferring infamy, threw himself into the hands of the English, offering to turn the kingdom over to the infant King Henry VI. (Henry V. having died).

Charles abandoned hope; how could he struggle against such a combination? He was considering whether he should find refuge in Spain or in Scotland, when the tide of events was turned by the strangest romance in history.

It must ever remain a mystery that a peasant girl, a child in years and in experience, should have believed herself called to such a mission; conferring only with her heavenly guides or "voices," that she should have sought the King, inspired him with faith in her, and in himself and his cause, reanimated the courage of the army, and led it herself to victory absolute and complete; and then, compelling the half-reluctant, half-doubting Charles to go with her to Rheims, where she had him anointed and consecrated, this simple child in that day bestowed upon him a kingdom, and upon France a King!

Was there ever a stranger chapter in history! Alas, if it could have ended here, and she could have gone back to her mother and her spinning and her simple pleasures, as she was always longing to do when her work should be done. But no! we see her falling into the hands of the defeated and revengeful English — this child, who had wrested from them a kingdom already in their grasp. She was turned over to the French ecclesiastical court to be tried. A sorceress and a blasphemer they pronounce her, and pass her on to the secular authorities, and her sentence is — death.

We see the poor defenceless girl, bewildered, terrified, wringing her hands and declaring her innocence as she rides to execution. God and man had abandoned her. No heavenly voice spoke, no miracle intervened as her young limbs were tied to the stake and the fagots and straw piled up about her. The torch was applied, and her pure soul mounted heavenward in a column of flames.

Rugged men wept. A Burgundian general said, as he turned gloomily away, "We have murdered a saint."

And Charles, sitting upon the throne she had rescued for him, what was he doing to save her? Nothing — to his everlasting shame be it said, nothing. He might not have succeeded; the effort at rescue, or to stay the event, might have been unavailing. But where was his knighthood, where his manhood, that he did not try, or utter passionate protest against her fate?

Twenty-five years later we see him erecting statues to her memory, and "rehabilitating" her desecrated name. And to-day, the Church which condemned her for blasphemy is placing her upon the calendar of saints, while all political parties alike are using her name as a thing to conjure with.

CHAPTER VII.

The early part of the sixteenth century must ever be memorable in the history of Europe. Ferdinand and Isabella had given to the human race a new world. Luther had hurled his defiance at Rome—had arraigned Leo X. for blasphemy and corrupt practices. Henry V., grandson of Ferdinand and Isabella (and nephew of Katharine, wife of Henry VIII.) was Emperor of Germany. Astute and powerful though he was, he had been unable to stay the Protestant flood. His empire, apparently hungering for the new heresy, was divided already into States Protestant and States Catholic. England was Protestant. The conversion of her King, because the Pope refused to annul his marriage with Katharine, was not one of the proudest triumphs of the new faith, but one of the most important. Had Katharine's charms been fresher, or Anne Boleyn's less alluring, the course of history might have been strangely changed. Henry VIII. as persecutor of heretics would have found congenial occupation for his ferocious instincts, and Protestantism would have been long delayed. Spain was unchangeably Catholic, while France offered congenial soil for the new faith. The germs of heresy, long slumbering, were everywhere stirred into life.

Francis I. was King; sumptuous in tastes, suave and elegant in manners, as handsome as an Apollo, gay, pleasure-loving, as vicious as he was false, and if need be with a cruelty which matched his ambition, such was the man who held the destinies of France at this time.

A rival claimant for the throne of Germany, he was destined to spend his life in fruitless contest with the more able, wily, and astute Henry V., the possession of that Empire the ignis-fatuus ever luring him on; an end to which all other ends were simply the means. The religious question upon which Europe was divided meant nothing to him, except as he could use it in his duel with the Emperor. He was in turn the ally of Henry VIII. or the willing tool of Henry V. If he needed the English King's friendship, the Protestants had protection. If he desired to placate Henry V., the roastings and torturings commenced again.

In 1547 Francis and Henry VIII. each went to his reward, and a few years later Henry V. had laid down his crown and carried his weary, unsatisfied heart to St. Yuste. The brilliant pageant was over; but Protestantism was expanding.

The question at issue was deeper than any one knew. Neither Luther nor Leo X. understood the revolution they had precipitated. Protestants and Papists alike failed to comprehend the true nature of the struggle, which was not for supremacy of Romanist or Protestant; not whether this dogma or that was true, and should prevail; but an assertion of the right of every human soul to choose its own faith and form of worship. The great battle for human liberty had commenced; the struggle for religious liberty was but the prelude to what was to follow. There was abundant proof later that Protestants no less than Papists needed only opportunity and power to be as cruel and intolerant as their persecutors had been. Before the Reformation was fifty years old, Servetus, one of the greatest men of his age, a scholar, philosopher, and man of irreproachable character, was burned at Geneva for heretical views concerning the nature of the Trinity, Calvin, the great organizer of Protestant theology, giving, if not the order for this crime, at least the nod of approval.

*****

Huguenot, that name of tragic association, was a corruption of the German *Eidgenossen* — meaning associates. By the way of Switzerland it came into France as *Eguenots*, and the transition to its present form was simple. The Huguenots were no longer a timorous band hiding in darkness as in the time of Francis I. A party with such leaders as Anthony de Bourbon, Prince of Condé (his brother), and Admiral Coligny, was not to be put down by a few roastings and stranglings here and there. Anthony de Bourbon (King of Navarre) was next in succession should the House of Valois become extinct, with a young son valiant as himself (the future Henry IV.) pressing on toward manhood.

Catholic France needed plenty of comfort from Rome and Madrid in dealing with this formidable body of heretics which had fastened upon her vitals, and which was in turn receiving aid and comfort from the young Protestant Queen across the Channel.

When that fair princess Catharine de Medici became the wife of Henry, second son of Francis I., no one suspected the tremendous import of the event. Powerless to win the affection or even confidence of her husband, she remained during his reign almost unobserved, but, as the event proved, not unobservant. Her alert faculties were not idle, and when upon the death of Henry II. she found herself Queen-Regent, with only a frail boy of sixteen to obstruct her will, she quickly gathered the threads she already knew so well, and her supple hand closed upon them with a grasp not to be relinquished while she lived.

Another young Princess had been tossed across the Channel. This time it was her most serene little highness, Marie Stuart, Queen of Scotland, intended for the dauphin, who was to be Francis II.

In order to be prepared for this high destiny, the little maid was brought when only six years old to the Court of France to be trained under the direct supervision of her future mother-in-law, Catharine de Medici. Poor little Marie Stuart — predestined to sin and to tragedy! Who could be good, with the blood of the Guises in her veins, and with Catharine de Medici as preceptress?

This marriage was planned before Catharine's advent to power, or it would never have been. Marie was the niece of the Duke of Guise, and the central thought of Catharine's policy was the exclusion of this ambitious, intriguing family from every avenue to power in the state. Now, Marie would be Queen, and who so natural advisers as her uncles of the house of "Lorraine"?

The marriage of the two children had taken place — the sickly boy with only a modest portion of intelligence was Francis II. Marie, his Queen, whom he adored, controlled him utterly, and was in turn controlled by her uncles, the Guises. The wily Catharine saw herself defeated by a beautiful girl of sixteen.

The family of Guise was the self-appointed head of the Catholic party in France and represented the most extreme views regarding the treatment of heretics. So the strange result was, that Catharine, if she looked for any allies in her fight with the house of Lorraine, of which the Duke of Guise was the head, must make common cause with the Protestants, whom she hated a little less than she did the uncles of Marie Stuart. But events were soon to change the situation. Did she hasten them? Such a suspicion may never have existed. But may one not suspect anything of a woman capable of a St. Bartholomew?

Francis II. was dead. Marie Stuart had passed out of French history. The fates were fighting on the side of Catharine, who wasted no regrets upon the death of a son, which made her Queen-Regent during the minority of her second son Charles. She entered upon her fight with the Guises with renewed energy, and became to some extent protector of the Protestants. Realizing that her time was brief, she prepared Charles for the position he would soon hold.

What can be said of a mother who seeks to exterminate every germ of truth or virtue in her son — who immerses him in degrading vices in order to deaden his too sensitive conscience and make him a willing tool for her purposes? Inheriting the splendid intelligence as well as genius for statecraft of the de Medici, nourished from her infancy upon Machiavellian principles, cold and cruel by nature, this Florentine woman has written her name in blood across the pages of French history.

CHAPTER VIII.

There is not time to tell the story of the events leading up to that fateful night, August 24, 1572. Impelled always by her fear and dread of the Guises, Catharine had been vacillating in her policy with the Huguenots. Charles IX. was now King: impressible, easily influenced, yet stubborn, intractable, incoherent, passionate, and unreliable; sometimes inclining to the Guises, sometimes to Coligny and the Huguenots, and always submitting at last after vain struggle to his imperious mother's will, in her efforts to free him from both. We see in him a weak character, not naturally bad, torn to distraction by the cruel forces about him, who when compelled to yield, as he always did in the end, to that terrible woman, would give way to fits of impotent rage against the fate which allowed him no peace.

A time arrived when Catharine feared the influence of the Protestant Coligny more than the Guises. Brave, patriotic, magnetic, he had succeeded in winning Charles' consent to declare war against Spain. Philip II. of Spain was Catharine's son-in-law and closest ally. Her entire policy would be undermined. At all hazards Coligny must be gotten rid of. The young King of Navarre, adored leader of the Protestants, was a constant menace; he too must in some way be disposed of.

There were sinister conferences with Philip of Spain and with his Minister, that incarnation of cruelty and of the Inquisition, the Duke of Alva.

God knows France was not guiltless in what followed; but the initiative, the inception of the horrid deed, was not French. It was conceived in the brain of either this Italian woman or her Spanish adviser and co-conspirator, the Duke of Alva. We will never know the inside history of the massacre of St. Bartholomew. It must ever remain a matter of conjecture just how and when it was planned, but the probabilities point strongly one way.

Charles was to be gradually prepared for it by his mother, the plot revealed to him as he was in condition to bear it; by working upon his fears, his suspicions, by stories of plottings against his life and his kingdom, to infuriate him, and then — before his rage was exhausted — to act. The marriage of Charles' sister Margaret with the young Protestant leader Henry of Navarre, with its promise of future protection to the Huguenots, was part of the plot. It would lure all the leaders of the cause to Paris. Coligny, Condé, all the heads of the party were urgently invited to attend the marriage-feast which was to inaugurate an era of peace.

Admiral Coligny was requested by Catharine, simply as a measure of protection to the Protestants, to have an additional regiment of guards in Paris, to act in case of any unforeseen violence.

Two days after the marriage and while the festivities were at their height, an attempt upon the life of the old Admiral awoke suspicion and alarm. But Catharine and her son went immediately in person to see the wounded old man, and to express their grief and horror at the event. They commanded that a careful list of the names and abode of every Protestant in Paris be made, in order, as they said, "to take them under their own immediate protection." "My dear father," said the King, "the hurt is yours, the grief is mine."

At that moment, the knives were already sharpened, every man instructed in his part in the hideous drama, and the signal for its commencement determined upon. Charles did not know it, but his mother did. She went to her son's room that night, artfully and eloquently pictured the danger he was in, confessed to him that she had authorized the attempt upon Coligny, but that it was done because of the Admiral's plottings against him, which she had discovered. But the Guises—her enemies and his—they knew it, and would denounce her and the King! The only thing now is to finish the work. He must die.

Charles was in frightful agitation and stubbornly refused. Finally with an air of offended dignity she bowed coldly and said to her son, "Sir, will you permit me to withdraw with my daughter, from your kingdom?" The wretched Charles was conquered. In a sort of insane fury he exclaimed, "Well, let them kill him, and all the rest of the Huguenots too. See that not one remains to reproach me."

This was more than she had hoped. All was easy now. So eager was she to give the order before a change of mood, that she flew herself to give the signal, fully two hours earlier than was expected. At midnight the tocsin rang out upon the night, and the horror began.

Lulled to a feeling of security by artfully contrived circumstances, husbands, wives, sons, daughters, peacefully sleeping, were awakened to see each other hideously slaughtered.

The stars have looked down upon some terrible scenes in Paris, her stones are not unacquainted with the taste of human blood, but never had there been anything like this. The carnage of battle is merciful compared with it. Shrieking women and children, half-clothed, fleeing from knives already dripping with human blood; frantic mothers shielding the bodies of their children, and wives pleading for the lives of husbands; the living hiding beneath the bodies of the dead.

The cry that ascended to Heaven from Paris that night was the most awful and despairing in the world's history. It was centuries of cruelty crowded into a few hours.

The number slain can never be accurately stated; but it was thousands. Human blood is intoxicating. An orgie set in which laughed at orders to cease. Seven days it continued and then died out for lack of material. The provinces had caught the contagion, and orders to slay were received and obeyed in all except two, the Governor of Bayonne, to his honor be it told, writing to the King in reply: "Your Majesty has many faithful subjects in Bayonne, but not one executioner."

And where was "His Majesty" while this work was being done? How was it with Catharine? She was possibly seeing to the embalming of Coligny's head, which we learn she sent as a present to the Pope. We hear of no regrets, no misgivings, that she was calm, collected, suave and unfathomable as ever, but that Charles in a strange, half-frenzied state was amusing himself by firing from the windows of the palace at the fleeing Huguenots. Had he killed himself in remorse, would it not have been better, instead of lingering two wretched years, a prey to mental tortures and an inscrutable malady, before he died?

Europe was shocked. Christendom averted her face in horror. But at Madrid and Rome there was satisfaction.

Catharine and the Duke of Alva had done their work skilfully, but the result surprised and disappointed them. Tens of thousands of Huguenots were slain, which was well; but many times that number remained, with spirit unbroken, which was not well.

They had been too merciful! Why had Henry of Navarre been spared? Had not Alva said, "Take the big fish and let the small fry go. One salmon is worth more than a thousand frogs."

But Charles considered the matter settled when he uttered those swelling words to Henry of Navarre the day after the massacre: "I mean in future to have one religion in my kingdom. It is mass or death."

Catharine's third son now wore the crown of France. In Henry III. she had as pliant an instrument for her will as in the two brothers preceding him; and, like them, his reign was spent in alternating conflict with the Protestants and the Duke de Guise. At last, wearied and exasperated, this half-Italian and altogether conscienceless King quite naturally thought of the stiletto. The old Duke, as he entered the King's apartment by invitation, was stricken down by assassins hidden for that purpose.

Henry had not counted on the rebound from that blow. Catholic France was excited to such popular fury against him that he threw himself into the arms of the Protestants, imploring their aid in keeping his crown and his kingdom; and when himself assassinated, a year later, in the absence of a son he named Henry, King of Navarre, his successor. A Protestant and a Huguenot was King of France.

CHAPTER IX.

After long wandering in strange seas, we come in view of familiar lights and headlands. With the advent of the house of Bourbon, we have grasped a thread which leads directly down to our own time.

The accession of a Protestant King was hailed with delirious joy by the Huguenots, and with corresponding rage by Catholic France. The one looked forward to redressing of wrongs and avenging of injuries; and the other flatly refused submission unless Henry should recant his heresy, and become a convert to the true faith.

The new King saw there was no bed of roses preparing for him. After four years of effort to reconcile the irreconcilable, he decided upon his course. He was not called to the throne to rule over Protestant France, nor to be an instrument of vengeance for the Huguenots. He saw that the highest good of the kingdom required, not that he should impose upon it either form of belief or worship, but give equal opportunity and privilege to both.

To the consternation of the Huguenots he announced himself ready to listen to the arguments in favor of the religion of Rome; and it took just five hours of deliberation to convince him of its truth. He announced himself ready to abjure his old faith. Bitter reproaches on the one side and rejoicings on the other greeted this decision. It was not heroic. But many even among the Protestants acknowledged it to be an act of supreme political wisdom.

Peace was restored, and the "Edict of Nantes," which quickly followed, proved to his old friends, the Huguenots, that they were not forgotten. The Protestants, with every disability removed, shared equal privileges with the Catholics throughout the kingdom; and the first victory for religious liberty was splendidly won.

An era of unexampled prosperity dawned. Never had the kingdom been so wisely and beneficently governed. Sincerity, simplicity, and sympathy had taken the place of dissimulation, craft, and cruelty. Uplifting agencies were everywhere at work, reaching even to the peasantry, that forgotten element in the nation.

The reign of the Bourbon dynasty had opened auspiciously. Henry IV. was the idol of the people. His loveless marriage with Margaret de Valois had been annulled, and he had espoused Marie de Medici. The blood from that poisoned stream was again to be intermingled with the blood of the future Kings of France.

After a reign of twenty-one years, the sagacious ruler who had done more than any other to make her great and happy was stricken down by the hand of an assassin, and a cry of grief arose alike from Catholic and Protestant throughout the kingdom.

Poor France was again at the mercy of a woman with the corrupt instincts of the de Medici. The widow of Henry IV., who was Regent during the infancy of her son Louis, was intriguing, vulgar, and without the ability of the great Catharine. The kingdom was rent by cabals of aspiring favorites and ambitious nobles, until the reign of Louis XIII., or rather of Cardinal Richelieu, began.

The foundations of this man's policy lay deep, out of sight of all save his own far-reaching intelligence. Pitiless as an iceberg, he crushed every obstacle to his purpose. Impartial as fate, with no loves, no hatreds, Catholics, Protestants, nobles, Parliaments, one after another were borne down before his determination to make the King, what he had not been since Charlemagne, supreme in France.

The will of the great minister mowed down like a scythe. The power of the grandees, that last remnant of feudalism, and a perpetual menace to monarchy, was swept away. One great noble after another was humiliated and shorn of his privileges, if not of his head.

The Huguenots, being first shaken into submission, saw their political liberties torn from them by the stroke of a pen, and even while the Catholics were making merry over this discomfiture, the minister was planning to send Henrietta, sister of the King, across the Channel to become Queen of Protestant England, as wife of Charles I. But the act of supreme audacity was to come. This high prelate of the church, this cardinal minister, formed alliance with Gustavus Adolphus, the great leader of the Protestants in the war upon the Emperor and the Pope!

He allowed no religion, no class, to sway or to hold him. He was for France; and her greatness and glory augmented under his ruthless dominion. By his extraordinary genius he made the reign of a commonplace King one of dazzling splendor; and while gratifying his own colossal ambition he so strengthened the foundations of the monarchy that princes of the blood themselves could not shake it.

It was great—it was dazzling, but of all his work there is but one thing which revolutions and time have not swept away. The "French Academy" alone survives as his monument. Out of a gathering of literary friends he created a national institution, its object the establishing a court of last appeal in all that makes for eloquence in speaking or writing the French language. In a country where nothing endures, this has remained unchanged for two hundred and thirty years.

But this master of statecraft, this creator of despotic monarchy, had one unsatisfied ambition. He would have exchanged all his honors for the ability to write one play like those of Corneille. Hungering for literary distinction, he could not have gotten into his own Academy had he not created it. And jealous of his laurels, he hated Corneille as much as he did the enemies of France.

CHAPTER X.

Again do we recognize the fine Italian hand in French politics. Cardinal Mazarin was Minister during the regency of Anne of Austria, directing and controlling the affairs of the Kingdom, less intent upon the greatness of France than the greatness and magnificence of her Prime Minister. At last the wily Italian was gone, and Louis XIV. settled himself upon the throne which Richelieu had rendered so exalted and immovable.

Cardinal Mazarin had said of the young Louis that "there was enough in him to make four Kings, and one honest man." His greatness consisted more in amplitude than in kind. Nature made him in prodigal mood. He was an average man of colossal proportions. His ability, courage, dignity, industry, greed for power and possessions, were all on a magnificent scale, and so were his vanity, his loves, his cruelties, his pleasures, his triumphs, and his disappointments.

No King more wickedly oppressed France, and none made her more glorious. He made her feared abroad and magnificent at home, but he desolated her, and drained her resources with ambitious wars. He crowned her with imperishable laurels in literature, art, and every manifestation of genius, but he signed the "Revocation of the Edict of Nantes," and drove out of his kingdom 500,000 of the best of his subjects.

If the names of Marlborough and Maintenon could have been stricken out of his life, the story might have had a different ending. From the moment the great Duke checked his victorious army, his sun began to go down; but it was Maintenon who most obscured its setting.

His unloved Queen, the Spanish Marie Therese, had borne his mad infatuation for Louise la Vallière; la Vallière had carried her broken heart to a convent, and been superseded by de Montespan, and de Montespan had invited her own destruction by bringing into her household the pious widow of the poet Scarron, Madame de Maintenon, (grand-daughter of d'Aubigne, the historian of the Reformation). Grave, austere, ambitious, talented, she was not too much engrossed in her duties as governess of de Montespan's children to find ways of establishing an influence over the King.

This man who had absorbed into himself all the functions of the Government, who was Ministers, Magistrates, Parliaments, all in one, this central sun of whom Corneille, Molière, Racine were but single rays, was destined to be enslaved in his old age by a designing adventuress; her will his law. The hey-day of youth having passed, he was beginning to be anxious about his soul. She artfully pricked his conscience, and de Montespan was sent away, but de Maintenon remained.

She next convinced him that the only fitting atonement for his sins was to drive heresy out of his kingdom, and re-establish the true faith. At her bidding he undid the glorious work of Henry IV., signed the "Revocation of the Edict of Nantes," and brutally stamped out Protestantism.

A part of the scheme of penitence seems to have been that on the death of poor Marie Therese, he should make her (de Maintenon) his lawful wife, which he did privately; and his sun went down obscured by crushing griefs and disappointments. His children swept away, the prestige of success tarnished, this demigod was taken to pieces by time's destroying fingers, quite as unceremoniously as are the rest of us, hiding finally behind the bed-curtains while a kneeling courtier passed to him his wig on the end of a stick, and at last lying down like any other old dying sinner, overwhelmed with the vanity of earthly things and with the vastness of eternity.

Still more would the dying moments of the Grand Monarque have been embittered could he have foreseen into what hands his great inheritance was passing.

Upon Louis XV. more than any other rests the responsibility of the crisis which was approaching.

A heartless sybarite, depraved in tastes, without sense of responsibility or comprehension of his times, a brutalized voluptuary governed by a succession of designing women, regardless of national poverty, indulging in wildest extravagance, — such was the man in whom was vested the authority rendered so absolute by Richelieu, — such the man who opened up a pathway for the storm.

As for the nobility, their degradation may be imagined when it is said there was as bitter rivalry between titled and illustrious fathers to secure for their daughters the coveted position held by Madame de Pompadour, as for the highest offices of State.

Could the upper ranks fall lower than this? Had not the kingdom reached its lowest depths, where its foreign policy was determined by the amount of consideration shown to Madame de Pompadour? But this woman, whose friendship was artfully sought by the great Empress Maria Theresa, was superseded, and the fresher charms of Madame du Barri enslaved the

King. The deposed favorite could not survive her fall, and died of a broken heart. It is said that as Louis, looking from an upper window of his palace, saw the coffin borne out in a drenching rain, he smiled and said: "Ah, the Marquise has a bad day for her journey." It may be imagined that the man who could be so pitiless to the woman he had loved would feel little pity for the people whom he had not loved, but whom he knew only as a remote, obscure something, which held up the weight of his glory.

But this "obscure something" was undergoing strange transformation. The greater light at the surface had sent some glimmering rays down into the mass below, which began to awaken and to think. Misery, hopeless and abject, was changing into rage and thirst for vengeance.

A new class had come into existence which was not noble, but with highly trained intelligence it looked with contempt and loathing upon the frivolous, half-educated nobles. Scorn was added to the ferment of human passions beneath the surface, and when Voltaire had spoken, and the restraints of religion were loosened, no living hand, not that of a Richelieu nor a Louis XIV., could have averted the coming doom. But—no one seems to have suspected what was approaching.

A wonderful literature had come into existence—not stately and classic as in the age preceding,—but instinct with a new sort of life. The highest speculations which can occupy the soul of man were handled with marvellous lightness of touch and prismatic brilliancy of expression; but all was negation. None tried to build; all to demolish. The black-winged angel of Destruction was hovering over the land.

Then Rousseau tossed his dreamy abstractions into the quivering air, and the formula, "Liberty, Fraternity, and Equality," was caught up by the titled aristocracy as a charming idyllic toy, while Princes, Dukes, and Marquises amused themselves with a dream of Arcadian simplicity, to be attained in some indefinite way in some remote and equally indefinite future. It was all a masquerade. No reality, no sincerity, no convictions, good or evil. The only thing that was real was that an over-taxed, impoverished people was exasperated and—hungry.

Did the King need new supplies for his unimaginable luxuries, they were taxed. Was it necessary to have new accessions to French "glory," in order to allay popular clamor or discontent, they must supply the men to fight the glorious battles, and the means with which to pay them. Every burden fell at last upon this lowest stratum of the State, the nobility and clergy, while owning two-thirds of the land, being nearly exempt from taxation.

And yet the King and nobility of France, in love with Rousseau's theories, were airily discussing the "rights of man." Wolves and foxes coming together to talk over the sacredness of the rights of property — or the occupants of murderers' row growing eloquent over the sanctity of human life! How incomprehensible that among those quick-witted Frenchmen there seems not one to have realized that the logical sequence of the formula, "Liberty, Fraternity, and Equality," must be, "Down with the Aristocrats!"

And so the surface which Richelieu had converted into adamant grew thinner and thinner each day, until King and Court danced upon a mere gilded crust, unconscious of the abysmal fires beneath. Some of those powdered heads fell into the executioner's basket twenty-five years later. Did they recall this time? Did Madame du Barri think of it, did she exult at her triumph over de Pompadour, when she was dragged shrieking and struggling to the guillotine?

And while France was thus weaving her future, what were the other nations doing? England, sane, practical, with little time for abstractions, and little said about "glory," was importing turnips, converting agriculture into a science, and under the instruction of exiled Huguenots, establishing marvellous industries. In the new kingdom of Prussia, a half-savage, half-inspired King had been importing artisans and skill of all sorts, reclaiming waste lands. Living like a miser, he had indulged in but one luxury: an army, which should be the best in the world. There was no powder, no patches at his Court; where he thrashed with his own royal hands male and female courtiers, starved, imprisoned, and cudgelled his son and heir to his throne for playing on the violin; and, it is said, so terrified and scarified his grenadiers with canes and cats that not one of them would not have preferred facing the enemy to meeting his enraged sovereign, had he done wrong.

Frederick was not a pleasant barbarian. But there is at least a ring of sincerity about all this, which it is refreshing to recall after the tinsel and depraved refinements of France under Louis XV., and something too which gives promise, in spite of its brutality, of a stalwart future.

Five years before the close of this miserable reign, an event occurred seemingly of small importance to Europe. A child was born in an obscure Italian household. His name was Napoleon Bonaparte.

CHAPTER XI.

Louis XV. was dead, and two children, with the light-heartedness of youth and inexperience, stepped upon the throne which was to be a scaffold — Louis XVI., only twenty, and Marie Antoinette, his wife, nineteen. He, amiable, kind, full of generous intentions; she, beautiful, simple, child-like and lovely. Instead of a debauched old King with depraved surroundings, here were a Prince and Princess out of a fairy-tale. The air was filled with indefinite promise of a new era for mankind to be inaugurated by this amiable young king, whose kindness of heart shone forth in his first speech, "We will have no more loans, no credit, no fresh burdens on the people;" then, leaving his ministers to devise ways of paying the enormous salaries of officials out of an empty treasury, and to arrange the financial details of his benevolent scheme of government, he proceeded with his gay and brilliant young wife to Rheims, there to be crowned with a magnificence undreamed of by Louis XIV.

In the midst of these rejoicings over the new reign, and of speculative dreams of universal freedom, there was wafted across the Atlantic news of a handful of patriots arrayed against the tyranny of the British Crown. Here were the theories of the new philosophy translated into the reality of actual experience. "No taxation without representation," "No privileged class," "No government without the consent of the governed." Was this not an embodiment of their dreams? Nor did it detract from the interest in the conflict that England — England, the hated rival of France, was defied by an indignant people of her own race. There was not a young noble in the land who would not have rushed if he could to the defence of the outraged colonies.

The King, half doubting, and vaguely fearing, was swept into the current, and the armies and the courage of the Americans were splendidly reinforced by generous, enthusiastic France.

Why should the simple-hearted Louis see what no one else seemed to see: that victory or failure were alike full of peril for France? If the colonies were conquered, France would feel the vengeance of England; if they were freed and self-governing, the principle of Monarchy had a staggering blow.

In the mean time, as the American Revolution moved on toward success, there was talk in the cabin as well as the *château* of the "rights of man." In shops and barns, as well as in clubs and drawing-rooms, there was a glimmering of the coming day.

"What is true upon one continent is true upon another," say they. "If it is cowardly to submit to tyranny in America, what is it in France?" "If Englishmen may revolt against oppression, why may not Frenchmen?" "No government without the consent of the governed, eh? When has our consent been asked, the consent of twenty-five million people? Are we sheep, that we have let a few thousands govern us for a thousand years, *without* our consent?"

Poverty and hunger gave force and urgency to these questions. The people began to clamor more boldly for the good time which had been promised by the kind-hearted King. The murmur swelled to an ominous roar. Thousands were at his very palace gates, telling him in no unmistakable terms that they were tired of smooth words and fair promises. What they wanted was a new constitution and — bread.

Poor Louis! the one could be made with pen and paper; but by what miracle could he produce the other? How gladly would he have given them anything. But what could he do? There was not enough money to pay the salaries of his officials, nor for his gay young Queen's fêtes and balls! The old way would have been to impose new taxes. But how could he tax a people crying at his gates for bread? He made more promises which he could not keep; yielded, one after another, concessions of authority and dignity; then vacillated, and tried to return over the slippery path, only to be dragged on again by an irresistible fate.

When Louis XVI. convoked the States-General, he made his last concession to the demands of his subjects.

That almost-forgotten body had not been seen since Richelieu effaced all the auxiliary functions of government. Nobles, ecclesiastics, and *tiers état* (or commons) found themselves face to face once more. The handsome contemptuous nobles, the princely ecclesiastics were unchanged — but there was a new expression in the pale faces of the commons. There was a look of calm defiance as they met the disdainful gaze of the aristocrats across the gulf of two centuries.

The two superior bodies absolutely refused to sit in the same room with the commons. They might under the same roof, but in the same room — never.

No outburst met this insult. With marvellous self-control and dignity, and with an ominous calm, the commons constituted themselves into the "National Assembly."

Aristocratic France had committed its concluding act of arrogance and folly. And when poor distracted Louis gave impotent order for the Assembly to disperse, he committed suicide. Louis the man lived on to be slain by the people three years later, but Louis the King died at that moment.

When the Assembly defied his authority and continued to solemnly act as if he had not spoken, the power had passed to the people. They were sovereign.

Paris was in wild excitement; and a rumor that troops were marching upon the Assembly to disperse it converted excitement into madness. The populace marched toward the Bastille, and in another hour the heads of the Governor and his officials were being carried on pikes through the streets of Paris.

The horrible drama had opened, and events developed with the swiftness of a falling avalanche. Louis might have followed his fleeing nobles. But always vacillating, and "letting I dare not wait upon I would," the opportunity was lost. He and his family were prisoners in the "Temple," while an awful travesty upon a court of justice was sending out death-warrants for his friends and adherents faster than the guillotine could devour them.

More and more furious swept the torrent, gathering to itself all that was vile and outcast. Where were the pale-faced, determined patriots who sat in the "National Assembly"? Some of them riding with Dukes and Marquises to the guillotine. Was this the equality they expected when they cried "Down with the Aristocrats"?

Did they think they could guide the whirlwind after raising it? As well whisper to the cyclone to level only the tall trees, or to the conflagration to burn only the temples and palaces.

With restraining agencies removed, religion, government, King, all swept away, that hideous brood born of vice, poverty, hatred, and despair came out from dark hiding-places; and what had commenced as a patriotic revolt had become a wild orgie of bloodthirsty demons, led by three master-demons, Robespierre, Marat, and Danton, vying with each other in ferocity.

Then we see that simple girl thinking by one supreme act of heroism and sacrifice, like Joan of Arc, to save her country. Foolish child! Did she think to slay the monster devouring Paris by cutting off one of his heads? The death of Marat only added to the fury of the tempest; and the falling of Charlotte Corday's head was not more noticed than the falling of a leaf in the forest.

On the 21st of January, 1793, Louis XVI. embraced for the last time his adored wife and children; then, with every possible indignity, was strapped to a plank and shoved under the guillotine.

The kindest-hearted, most inoffensive gentleman in Europe had expiated the crimes of his ancestors.

A few months later, Marie Antoinette, daughter of the proud Empress Maria Theresa, and child of the Cæsars, was borne along the same road. And how bravely she met her awful fate! We forget her follies, her reckless grasping after pleasures, in view of her horrible sufferings and in admiration of her courage as she rides to her death; sitting in that hideous tumbril, head erect, pale, proud, defiant, as if upon a throne.

With the death of the King and Queen the madness had reached its height, and a revulsion of feeling set in. There was a surfeit of blood, and an awakening sense of horror, which turned upon the instigators. Danton fell, and finally, when amid cries of "Death to the tyrant!" Robespierre was dragged wounded and shivering to the fate he had brought upon so many thousands, the drama which had opened at the Bastille was fittingly closed.

The great battle for human liberty had been fought and won. Religious freedom and political freedom were identical in principle. The right of the human conscience proclaimed by Luther in 1517 had in 1793 only expanded into the large conception of all the inherent rights of the *individual*.

It had taken centuries for English persistence to accomplish what France, with such appalling violence, had done in as many years. It had been a furious outburst of pent-up force; but the work had been thorough. Not a germ of tyranny remained. The incrustations of a thousand years were not alone broken, but pulverized; the privileged classes were swept away, and their vast estates, two-thirds of the territory of France, ready to be distributed among the rightful owners of the soil, those who by toil and industry could win them. France was as new as if she had no history. There was ample opportunity for her people now. What would they do with it?

CHAPTER XII.

It is strange to read that the armies went on fighting battles automatically, even while there was no central head to direct them. While the ghastly scenes were enacting in Paris, and while Josephine de Beauharnais was at the Conciergerie listening with blanched face to the call of her husband's name on the death roll for the day, a young lieutenant of artillery, only twenty-four years old, was at Toulon, winning his first military honors. He would have been thought a strange prophet who had said that in less than ten years the young Corsican lieutenant would be Emperor, and the prisoner at the Conciergerie Empress of the French! Nor did M. de Beauharnais, as he rode to execution, dream that forty-five years later his grandson would over the same stones be borne to his coronation.

In the anarchy which prevailed after the Revolution, the young hero of Toulon was called upon to quell a riot in Paris. The people realized they had met a master. For twenty-five years from that day, the history of France, and indeed of Europe, was that of one man, Napoleon Bonaparte. Commander-in-chief of the Army, then First Consul of the Republic, then Emperor — the steps in his ascent were as rapid and as bewildering as the movements in one of his own campaigns. France, groping about helplessly among the wreckage of the past, believed what she most desired was *liberty* and *self-government*.

This Italian, who was a French citizen even only by merest accident, knew her better than she did herself, and that what she really wanted was a fresh mantle of glory to cover her humiliation, and — a master.

Leading a broken, unpaid, half-clothed army into Italy, he electrified France and all Europe. Before the world had really found out who he was, and whence he had come, he had conquered all of Northern Italy, part of Austria and Belgium, had created a Cisalpine Republic out of the fragments, and was making treaties and dictating terms to kings and princes.

France, discredited and almost disgraced among the monarchies of Europe, found herself suddenly feared and glorious. Napoleon had captured the most imaginative and military people in Europe. The rest of the way was easy. Prudent, discreet, knowing when to wait, and when to come down like an avalanche, this marvellous man held France in his hands, and placed Europe under his feet.

The people which had exerted such superhuman effort for freedom were held by a hand more despotic than Richelieu's, more destructive to popular freedom than that of Louis XIV.; and the more absolute his rule, the more overpowering his authority, the better pleased they seemed to be.

But, was there not equal opportunity for every man in the Empire? Every soldier's knapsack, might it not hold a Marshal's baton? Was not the Emperor himself a living illustration of what a man from the people might become? And then what did it mean to Frenchmen to be suddenly lifted to dazzling ascendancy in Europe? Who would not willingly serve a master who could bring Hapsburg, Hohenzollern, Romanoff, Bourbon, crouching at his feet—who could tear down states, and set them up, and if an extra throne were needed for a retainer, could carve a new state from territory of friend and foe alike, and place a diadem upon every head in his domestic or military household? It was the most stupendous display of personal power ever beheld, England alone standing upright in his presence, and in the end accomplishing his ruin.

When Austria with a reluctant shudder bestowed her princess upon the invincible parvenu, and when France with regretful pity saw the adored Josephine set aside for that disdainful royal maiden, Marie Louise, at that moment Napoleon passed the meridian of his greatness.

It had taken just fifteen years to make the most astonishing and dazzling chapter in French history; and then came "Moscow" and "Elba," to be quickly followed by "Waterloo" and "St. Helena." And then for France— most incomprehensible of all—a return to the Bourbons! It had required the greatest tragedy of modern times to get rid of them, and here they were again, Louis XVIII. and Charles X., as overbearing and as arrogant as if their brother's head had not dropped into a basket in 1793. When somebody said of the Bourbons "they learn nothing and forget nothing," he was inaccurate. They had certainly forgotten the French Revolution.

But death removed the first, and popular sentiment the second, of these relics of an obsolete past. And a new experiment was tried. This time it was the son of *Philippe Egalité*, that wickedest of all the regicides, who came smiling and bowing before the people as a popular sovereign, who would beneficently rule under a liberal constitution. Whatever his father had been, Louis Philippe was far from being a wicked man. Whether teaching school in Switzerland, or giving French lessons in America, or wearing the kingly crown in France, he was the kindest hearted, most inoffensive of gentlemen.

When in the pre-revolutionary days we read of France making war, it means that the King, or his minister, with more or less deference to the will of a few thousand nobles, did so. They are the France referred to. The real France was not consulted and had nothing to do with it, unless it were to fill the ranks with fathers, sons, and husbands, and then pay the taxes imposed to support them. But times were changed. Under a constitutional monarchy, the King does not govern; he reigns. Louis Philippe was King of the French, — not of France. He was chosen by the people as their ornamental figurehead. But what if he ceased to be ornamental? What was the use of a King who in eighteen years had added not a single ray of glory to the national name, but who was using his high position to increase his enormous private fortune, and incessantly begging an impoverished country for benefits and emoluments for five sons?

An excellent father, truly, though a short-sighted one. His power had no roots. The cutting from the Orleans tree had never taken hold upon the soil, and toppled over at the sound of Lamartine's voice proclaiming a Republic from the balcony of the "Hôtel de Ville."

When invited to step down from his royal throne, he did so on the instant. Never did King succumb with such alacrity, and never did retiring royalty look less imposing, than when Louis Philippe was in hiding at Havre under the name of "William Smith," waiting for safe convoy to England, without having struck one blow in defence of his throne.

But three terrible words had floated into the open windows of the Tuileries. With the echoes of 1792 still sounding in his ears, "Liberty," "Fraternity," and "Equality," shouted in the streets of Paris, had not a pleasant sound!

Republicanism was an abiding sentiment in France, even while two dull Bourbon Kings were stupidly trying to turn back the hands on the dial of time, and while an Orleans, with more supple neck, was posing as a popular sovereign. During all this tiresome interlude, the real fact was developing. A Republican sentiment which had existed vaguely in the air was materializing, consolidating, into a more and more tangible reality in the minds of thinking men and patriots.

The ablest men in the country stood with plans matured, ready to meet this crisis. A Republic was proclaimed; M. de Lamartine, Ledru-Rollin, General Cavaignac, M. Raspail, and Louis Napoleon were rival candidates for the office of President.

The nephew of Napoleon Bonaparte, and son of Hortense, was only known as the perpetrator of two very absurd attempts to overthrow the monarchy under Louis Philippe. But since the remains of the great Emperor had been returned to France by England, and the splendors of the past placed in striking contrast with a dull, lustreless present, there had been a revival of Napoleonic memories and enthusiasm. Here was an opportunity to unite two powerful sentiments in one man—a Napoleon at the head of Republican France would express the glory of the past and the hope of the future.

The magic of the name was irresistible. Louis Napoleon was elected President of the second Republic, and history prepared to repeat itself. What sort of a ruler would he be—this dark, mysterious, unmagnetic man? Even should he not turn out well, no great harm could be done. It was only for four years. His hand had not the steely fineness of touch of his great uncle's, but it was strong, and guided, they soon found, by a subtle intelligence.

The overthrow of Monarchy in France had set fire to Republicanism in Europe, Kossuth with transcendent eloquence leading a revolution in Hungary, and Garibaldi and Mazzini with pen and sword in Italy. Europe was in a blaze of revolt. The first great military exploit of Napoleon Bonaparte had been in Italy, and so was his nephew's, but with this difference—the object of the one was to build up Republics on the other side of the Alps, and of the other to pull them down. Garibaldi and Mazzini were driven out of Italy by French bayonets, which also propped up the pontifical throne for the fugitive Pope.

The Assembly soon realized that in this Prince-President it had no automaton to deal with. A deep antagonism grew, and the cunningly devised issue could not fail to secure popular support to Louis Napoleon. When an Assembly is at war with the President because it desires to restrict the suffrage, and he to make it universal, can any one doubt the result? He was safe in appealing to the people on such an issue, and sure of being sustained in his Proclamation dissolving the Assembly. He was gathering the reins into his hands with the astute courage of his uncle. Moving on almost identical lines with his great original, the nephew set his face toward the same goal.

The French people must have realized they were being betrayed. They must have seen that this ambitious plotter was slipping the old fetters of arbitrary power into position. But, under the powerful spell of the Napoleonic name, lulled to tranquillity by the gift of suffrage, and fascinated by the growing splendors of an ingenious reproduction of the most brilliant chapter in French history, they were unresistingly drawn into the Imperial net.

France was for the second time an Empire, and Napoleon III. was Emperor of the French.

His Mephistophelian face did not look as classic under the laurel wreath as had his uncle's, nor had his work the blinding splendor nor the fineness of texture of his great model. But then, an imitation never has. It was a marble masterpiece, done in plaster! But what a clever reproduction it was! And how, by sheer audacity, it compelled recognition and homage, and at last even adulation in Europe!—and what a clever stroke it was, for this heavy, unsympathetic man to bring up to his throne from the people a radiant Empress, who would capture romantic and æsthetic France!

The distance was great from cheap lodgings in New York to a seat upon the Imperial throne of France; but human ambition is not easily satisfied. A Pelion always rises beyond an Ossa. It was not enough to feel that he had re-established the prosperity and prestige of France, that fresh glory had been added to the Napoleonic name. Was there not after all a certain irritating reserve in the homage paid him, was there not a touch of condescension in the friendship of his royal neighbors? And had he not always a Mordecai at his gate—while the *"Faubourg St. Germain"* stood aloof and disdainful, smiling at his brand-new aristocracy?

War is the thing to give solidity to empire and to reputation! Neither France nor Europe can withstand the magic of military renown. And so, upon a quickly improvised pretext, the French Emperor started, amid the booming of cannon and the wild acclamations of a delighted people, upon his errand of conquest. The insolent Germans were to be chastised; and, incidentally, Europe was to be made to tremble!

In a few months the bubble was pricked. The glittering French army proved to be a thing of tinsel and fustian. No reality, no power to stand before the solid German battalions, it melted like hoar-frost. Napoleon III. was prisoner of war at Sedan, and King William, Unser Fritz, and Von Moltke were at Versailles.

Moved by his colossal misfortunes, and perhaps partly in displeasure at having a French Republic once more at her door, England offered asylum to the deposed Emperor. There, from the seclusion of "Chiselhurst," he and his still beautiful Eugenie watched the Republic weathering the first days of storm and stress, and coming out at last stable and triumphant.

The weary exile felt that not in his day would the reaction come. But his son would yet wear the Imperial crown which was his birthright. Futile dream! The boy was destined to cruel fate—to be slain by Zulu assegai, while fighting the battles of England,—England, the author of *Waterloo*. Strange ending for the heir to the name and glory of Napoleon Bonaparte.

But the reaction Louis Napoleon so confidently hoped for did not come. With military pride humbled in the dust, national pride wounded by the loss of two provinces, loaded down with an immense war indemnity, the people set about the task of rehabilitation; in an incredibly short time, the galling debt was paid, financial prosperity and political strength restored, and with military organization second to none in Europe, France, with revengeful eyes fastened on Germany, waits for the day of reckoning.

For twenty-four years the Republic has existed. Communistic fires always smouldering have again and again burst forth — demagogues, fanatics, and those creatures for whom there is no place in organized society, whose element is chaos, standing ready to fan the fires of revolt; while Orleanist, Bonapartist, Bourbon, are ever on the alert, watching for opportunity to slip in through the open door of Revolution.

England in conscious superiority smiles at a nation which has had seven political revolutions in a hundred years. Republic, then Empire, then a return to the Bourbons, then Constitutional Monarchy under Louis Philippe, then Republic, followed by Empire again, and now for the third time a Republic!

But France, complex, mobile, changeful as the sea, in riotous enjoyment of her new-found liberties, casts off a form of government as she would an ill-fitting garment. She knows the value of tranquillity — she had it for one thousand years! The *people*, which have only breathed the upper air for a century — the people, who were stifled under feudalism, stamped upon by Valois Kings, riveted down by Richelieu, then prodded, outraged, and starved by Bourbons, have become a great nation. Many-sided, resourceful, gifted, it matters not whether they have called the head of their government Consul, Emperor, King, or President. They are a race of freemen, who can never again be enslaved by tyrannous system.

It was a bright day for France when that ambitious young Emperor of Germany sent his great Chancellor into retirement; and another bright day when, taking offence at scant courtesy at the hands of the Czar, he left ajar the back door to his dominions. An alliance between despotic Russia thirsting for the waters of the Mediterranean, and Republican France thirsting for revenge, is the darkest cloud on the German horizon to-day. It is only a matter of months or of years when France will be at the throat of Germany demanding Alsace and Lorraine. The French army is not the one which faced Von Moltke in 1871; and when France knocks at her front door, Germany will have all she can attend to, without hearing Russian batteries thundering at her rear. A dramatic reconciliation with the old Chancellor is interesting, but it will not undo the work of the last four years.

There is no longer thought of conflict between any two nations of Europe. The next war is to be one of tremendous combinations. National alliances are shifting and uncertain. But at the time this is written (1894) Germany, Austria, and Italy are drawn together in one hostile camp, while France and Russia, in loving embrace, stand in the other; and England, aloof and suspicious, holds herself ready to hurl her weight against whichever one obstructs her path to India.

There is something in the air which makes one think the name Napoleon is still a thing to conjure with. But whatever the future may hold for France, no American can be indifferent to the fate of a nation to whom we owe so much. Nor can we ever forget that in the hour of our direst extremity, and regardless of cost to herself, she helped us to establish our liberties, and to take our place among the great nations of the earth.